The Li·
of Tuff Spot Activities

Fun in a Builder's Tray

by Ruth Ludlow
Illustrations by Kerry Ingham

LITTLE BOOKS WITH BIG IDEAS

This 2nd edition published 2013 by Featherstone Education
an imprint of Bloomsbury Publishing Plc
50 Bedford Square, London, WC1B 3DP
www.bloomsbury.com

Bloomsbury is a registered trademark of Bloomsbury Publishing Plc

ISBN 978-1-4729-0733-2

First published in the UK by Featherstone Education, 2006

Printed and bound in India by Replika Press Pvt Ltd

This book is produced using paper that is made from wood grown in managed,
sustainable forests. It is natural, renewable and recyclable.

The logging and manufacturing processes conform to the environmental
regulations of the country of origin.

3 5 7 9 10 8 6 4 2

**To see our full range of titles
visit www.bloomsbury.com/featherstone**

Contents

Introduction

This book is one of the titles in a series of Little Books, which explore aspects of practice within the Early Years Foundation Stage in England. The books are also suitable for practitioners working with the early years curriculum in Wales, Northern Ireland and Scotland, and in any early years setting catering for young children.

Across the series you will find titles appropriate to each aspect of the curriculum for children from two to five years, giving practitioners a wealth of ideas for engaging activities, interesting resources and stimulating environments to enrich their work across the early years curriculum.

Each title also has information linking the activity pages to the statutory early years curriculum for England. This title has been updated to include the revised Early Learning Goals published by the Department for Education in March 2012. The full set of 19 goals is included in the introduction to each book, and the activity pages will refer you to the relevant statements to which each activity contributes.

For the purposes of observation and assessment of the children's work in each activity, we recommend that practitioners should use each of the 'revised statements' as a whole, resisting any impulse to separate the elements of each one into short phrases.

The key goals for this title are highlighted in purple, although other goals may be included on some pages.

PRIME AREAS

Communication and language

1 Listening and attention: children listen attentively in a range of situations. They listen to stories, accurately anticipating key events and respond to what they hear with relevant comments, questions or actions. They give their attention to what others say and respond appropriately, while engaged in another activity.

2 Understanding: children follow instructions involving several ideas or actions. They answer 'how' and 'why' questions about their experiences and in response to stories or events.

3 Speaking: children express themselves effectively, showing awareness of listeners' needs. They use past, present and future forms accurately when talking about events that have happened or are to happen in the future. They develop their own narratives and explanations by connecting ideas or events.

Physical development

1 **Moving and handling**: children show good control and co-ordination in large and small movements. They move confidently in a range of ways, safely negotiating space. They handle equipment and tools effectively, including pencils for writing.

2 **Health and self-care**: children know the importance for good health of physical exercise, and a healthy diet, and talk about ways to keep healthy and safe. They manage their own basic hygiene and personal needs successfully, including dressing and going to the toilet independently.

Personal, social and emotional development

1 **Self-confidence and self-awareness**: children are confident to try new activities, and say why they like some activities more than others. They are confident to speak in a familiar group, will talk about their ideas, and will choose the resources they need for their chosen activities. They say when they do or don't need help.

2 **Managing feelings and behaviour**: children talk about how they and others show feelings, talk about their own and others' behaviour, and its consequences, and know that some behaviour is unacceptable. They work as part of a group or class, and understand and follow the rules. They adjust their behaviour to different situations, and take changes of routine in their stride.

3 **Making relationships**: children play co-operatively, taking turns with others. They take account of one another's ideas about how to organise their activity. They show sensitivity to others' needs and feelings, and form positive relationships with adults and other children.

SPECIFIC AREAS

Literacy

1 **Reading**: children read and understand simple sentences. They use phonic knowledge to decode regular words and read them aloud accurately. They also read some common irregular words. They demonstrate understanding when talking with others about what they have read.

2 **Writing**: children use their phonic knowledge to write words in ways which match their spoken sounds. They also write some irregular common words. They write simple sentences which can be read by themselves and others. Some words are spelt correctly and others are phonetically plausible.

Mathematics

1 Numbers: children count reliably with numbers from 1 to 20, place them in order and say which number is one more or one less than a given number. Using quantities and objects, they add and subtract two single-digit numbers and count on or back to find the answer. They solve problems, including doubling, halving and sharing.

2 Shape, space and measures: children use everyday language to talk about size, weight, capacity, position, distance, time and money to compare quantities and objects and to solve problems. They recognise, create and describe patterns. They explore characteristics of everyday objects and shapes and use mathematical language to describe them.

Understanding the world

1 People and communities: children talk about past and present events in their own lives and in the lives of family members. They know that other children don't always enjoy the same things, and are sensitive to this. They know about similarities and differences between themselves and others, and among families, communities and traditions.

2 The world: children know about similarities and differences in relation to places, objects, materials and living things. They talk about the features of their own immediate environment and how environments might vary from one another. They make observations of animals and plants and explain why some things occur, and talk about changes.

3 Technology: children recognise that a range of technology is used in places such as homes and schools. They select and use technology for particular purposes.

Expressive arts and design

1 Exploring and using media and materials: children sing songs, make music and dance, and experiment with ways of changing them. They safely use and explore a variety of materials, tools and techniques, experimenting with colour, design, texture, form and function.

2 Being imaginative: children use what they have learnt about media and materials in original ways, thinking about uses and purposes. They represent their own ideas, thoughts and feelings through design and technology, art, music, dance, role-play and stories.

All the ideas in this book involve using a 'Tuff Spot'. A Tuff Spot is a square or octagonal shallow plastic tray, usually used for mixing cement. Tuff Spots (sometimes called builders' trays) are inexpensive and can be obtained from most large DIY stores or builders' merchants. You can also buy trays from educational suppliers. TTS (**www.tts-group.co.uk**) sell them, and have different sizes and types, including one with a mirrored surface.

You can also get a stand for the Tuff Spot, but a table will be much more flexible. For much of the time the Tuff Spot will be used on the floor indoors or the ground outside.

If you are unable to afford a Tuff Spot, you could use an existing water or sand tray, or a large plastic box. Most of the activities in this book can be done in a smaller tray, but the scope for imagination in play may be restricted.

The advantage of Tuff Spots is that they are so versatile. They are light enough for the children to transport almost anywhere, indoors and outdoors, and the low sides can contain the messiest of activities whilst allowing the children to get right into the thick of things.

Cleaning a Tuff Spot is no problem; leave it outside until you are ready to clean it, then help the children to pour warm soapy water all over it. A final scrub with a washing up brush or some big sponges will finish the job, and the children love doing it!

Storage is easy too. A Tuff Spot will slide behind cupboard, under a shelf, at the side of a shed and, if you have more than one, they stack easily and neatly, taking up very little space. These versatile surfaces can be used for many activities, both child-initiated and adult directed, and we have tried to present the ideas in this book in a way that will enable the widest range of uses.

Health and safety

Some of the activities in this book involve using foodstuffs and making things to eat. If you are using these activities you will need two Tuff Spots, one that is available for general everyday uses, the other that is **only** used for food. Remember the rules about food hygiene and follow the guidance in your setting for equipment used for cooking and food preparation.

Guidance on looking after a 'food based' Tuff Spot:

▶ buy it specially and never use it for other sorts of play (not even dough play!)

▶ keep it in a plastic bag or covered with a plastic sheet

▶ clean it carefully before and after every use

▶ make sure children wash their hands before using this tray

▶ explain to children and other adults why this tray is special; you may want to mark it in some way so it is not used by mistake.

Additional resources

The catalogues of some educational suppliers contain resources to use with a Tuff Spot, and these include mats for the base, which turn it into a beach, farm, zoo moonscape, etc. Of course, these resources may have appeal because they save time and planning. However, the children will have a much richer experience if you use a wide variety of resources to create your own ideas and activities using the pages in this book as starting points. In this way the Tuff Spot becomes a more sensory and tactile experience, as well as providing a springboard for much wider experiences.

Using this book

Each page in this book follows the same structure. There is clear guidance on what you might need when setting up the activity, and how this might be presented to groups of children. Of course, younger children may need a different range of materials from older children.

Our illustrator has shown each Tuff Spot in a 'ready to go' state. You will find different ways of presenting the materials you have collected; whether to offer the play indoors or outdoors; on a table or on the floor; everything available or just a small starter, with more to come later. The activity will work best if you involve the children, wherever possible, in planning and organising the activity and resources.

We have given an indication of the broad areas of learning and the aspects within these which the activity may cover. However, the children's play may very well take them into other areas of learning, gaining the use of different skills, vocabulary or new knowledge that you had not necessarily planned.

The preparatory activities can be linked with or inspired by other work going on in your setting. Sometimes we have suggested a book, a walk, or a discussion.

Sometimes we have just suggested that you draw children's attention to everyday objects or things that happen. This focusing of attention is often all you need to make the activity relevant to children when you set up the Tuff Spot and its contents.

Each activity starts with a period of child-initiated and chosen play with the materials you have collected. Through self-initiated play, children will become familiar with the materials, in preparation for the more focused activities you may embark on later. This stage of play needs careful observation and support, and may influence what you do next - including adjusting or adapting your planning to make sure the activity continues to be matched to the needs of the children in your setting.

Following this section are some ideas for adult led or adult directed activities. These are just suggestions. You may think of more, and the children you work with may suggest extensions themselves. Adult led activities need to follow plenty of child-initiated sessions. Don't rush into this section!

The final section on each double page spread contains other linked ideas, websites, resources and further activities that might follow your initial sessions.

Tuff Spot activities can provide wonderful experiences in every area of learning. They are easy to set up, need relatively simple everyday objects, can be used anywhere, and can sometimes be just the thing to spark interest in children who are difficult to motivate or inspire.

Images and Internet links

Publisher's note on using the Internet:
In this book we have included some suggestions for searches for images and websites. We advise practitioners that children should never be left unattended when searching for images or information on the Internet.

Autumn sculpture

Focus

Add value to a seasonal walk by offering further creative play with found items.

What you need:

Treasures from an autumn walk:

▶ acorns, conkers, leaves

▶ twigs, fir cones, soil

▶ pebbles and stones

▶ digital camera, magnifying glasses

Contribution to Early Learning Goals

PRIME

Communication and language ① ② ③
Physical development ① ②
PSED ③

SPECIFIC

Mathematics ① ②
Knowledge of the world ① ② ③
Expressive arts and design ① ②

What you do:

1. Take the children on a walk, making sure you follow your setting's guidance for health and safety and risk analysis. If a walk is not possible, ask the children to bring objects they have collected from their gardens, from the walk to school or from family walks. (Providing every child with their own bag or box for objects is a good way of stimulating interest, either on a group walk or when children are collecting at home.)

2. Put some damp soil in a Tuff Spot. Leave the soil in a pile for the children to arrange.

3. You could set out a few objects, ready for children who may not have their own collection.

Independent exploration

▶ Leave the Tuff Spot for children to play with, using their own collections of objects to make patterns, paths, sculptures or maps. Make sure they have plenty of time to explore the things they have collected. Offer the camera so they can photograph their creations.

Ideas for adult-initiated activities

▶ Look at pictures and books about autumn. Try putting 'Andy Goldsworthy' in Google to find some creations by an artist who works with natural materials.

▶ Look at the objects closely through magnifying glasses, and discuss what you see. Look at the fronts and backs of leaves, the patterns in stones, bark textures, skeleton leaves.

▶ Look for tiny insects that may have been collected too. Can the children identify these?

▶ Give the children spoken instructions of how to arrange the objects. 'Put three leaves next to the grey stone.' 'Put an acorn under the biggest green leaf.' 'Choose the biggest leaf and put it on top of the biggest stone.' etc.

And another idea...

After all the children have made and photographed their creations, put some paint and brushes with the autumn collection. They will thoroughly enjoy giving their objects a new look. Most children will find this gives a whole new direction to the activity.

Squirting Elmer

Focus

Water, straws and food colouring bring a familiar story to life while washing an elephant!

What you need:

- ▶ plastic straws, all sizes
- ▶ food colouring (optional)
- ▶ bubble mixture or washing-up liquid
- ▶ the story of 'Elmer the Patchwork Elephant'
- ▶ small world animals
- ▶ paint and brushes

Contribution to Early Learning Goals

PRIME
Communication and language ① ② ③
Physical development ①
PSED ① ② ③

SPECIFIC
Literacy ①
Knowledge of the world ① ② ③
Expressive arts and design ① ②

What you do:

1. Working with straws is quite difficult for some children, as they often suck when they should blow! Cut a small nick in each straw, about 1 inch from the top, using a sharp knife or scissors; this will stop them drinking too much of the water. In the interests of hygiene, each child should have their own straw.

2. Fill the Tuff Spot with water and add a few drops of food colouring if you like.

3. Show the children which end of the straw to blow down.

Independent exploration

▶ Leave the Tuff Spot and water for experimenting. Offer the camera so they can photograph their creations and each other.

Ideas for adult-initiated activities

▶ Read the story of 'Elmer the Patchwork Elephant', and talk about what happened when the elephants painted themselves and then got wet. Then you could paint some small world animals (including elephants) and wash them by spraying them through the straws.

▶ Add some washing up liquid to the water and see what happens now when they blow down the straws, and when they wash the animals. Talk about why the bubbles last longer and get bigger with washing up liquid, and why the washing is easier. Relate this to why we use washing up liquid for dirty dishes!

▶ If you can do this activity outside in the sunlight, look at the bubbles as they float away, and talk about the colours, sizes and shapes.

▶ Add some liquid paint to the water and make some bubble patterns or pictures.

▶ Make a car wash for toy cars, or a bubble bath for dolls. Use the straws to wash and rinse the objects in the Tuff Spot.

And another idea...

Explore small, hand-held sprays (the sort used for house plants and gardens) to spray water or dilute paint on big sheets of paper flat on the ground or pinned to an outside wall.

Google search: 'elephants' or 'elephant sculpture'.

Tracking colours

Focus

Use toy cars to make tracks, patterns and trails in sand, mud, paint or other substances.

What you need:

▶ fairly thick paint, several colours

▶ toy cars, diggers and other vehicles

▶ a small bucket or bowl of water

Contribution to Early Learning Goals

PRIME

Communication and language ① ② ③
Physical development ①
PSED ① ② ③

SPECIFIC

Literacy ②
Knowledge of the world ① ②
Expressive arts and design ① ②

What you do:

1. Use opportunities when you are out of doors to look for tracks and trails, for example:

   ▷ footprints on a path near a puddle

   ▷ boot prints in the mud on a rainy day

   ▷ bird prints in the garden

   ▷ car tyres on a road.

2. Squirt or spoon two or three pools of paint onto the Tuff Spot. Choose colours that contrast well with the Tuff Spot colour. Put a basket of toy cars nearby for free play.

3. Add a bucket of soapy water for rinsing the cars if their wheels get very painty.

Independent exploration

▶ Leave the Tuff Spot for children to play with, using the cars to make tracks and trails in the paint. Offer to wash the Tuff Spot if the paint gets very messy or the colours go muddy – however, some children like this better!

Ideas for adult-initiated activities

▶ Join the children in their play and talk about the tracks and trails. Remind them of the ones they see in real life. Look at the different tracks made by different vehicles.

▶ Clean the Tuff Spot, and then work together with a few simple blobs of colour and sticks or brushes to explore how colours change as they are mixed. Get the children to predict before they start, what will happen to red and yellow, blue and red, blue and yellow, black and white, red and white. Wash the surface regularly to keep the colours clear.

▶ Hands and fingers can also be used to mix paint, or try mixing with bare feet and making footprints with the mixtures.

And another idea...

Put a shallow layer (about 5cm/2") of soil, gravel or damp sand in the Tuff Spot for different tracks and trails. Experiment with prints of different objects – a basket of children's shoes, some construction pieces (Lego, Sticklebricks etc), a few kitchen implements (a potato masher, a sieve).

Google search: 'amazing textures' for free downloads of lots of surface textures.

Five a day

Focus

Explore different fruits and vegetables, then use them for artistic activities.

If the children are going to eat food used for this activity, use a 'for food' Tuff Spot. See guidance on page 8.

What you need:

▶ fruit and vegetables with different shapes, textures and colours

▶ suitable children's knives, forks and peelers

▶ magnifying glasses

▶ digital camera

Contribution to Early Learning Goals

PRIME

Communication and language ① ② ③
Physical development ① ②
PSED ① ② ③

SPECIFIC

Mathematics ① ②
Knowledge of the world ②
Expressive arts and design ① ②

What you do:

If the children are going to explore the fruit and vegetables before using them to create designs and patterns, look for seasonal varieties that will be less expensive and wasteful – or ask a local greengrocer or market trader for produce that is near the end of its 'shelf life'. This will reduce waste and remind children that food is important! Some fruits and vegetables you might consider as well as the more familiar ones are: watermelons, marrows, potatoes, onions, leeks, cooking apples, a coconut, pomegranates, tomatoes, peas in their shells, peppers.

1. Put the fruit/vegetables in the clean Tuff Spot. Adding some forks, children's knives, peelers etc. Keep some pieces on one side so they are clean for tasting later. You could read a story such as 'Oliver's Vegetables' or 'Oliver's Fruit Salad' as an introduction to the activity.

Independent exploration

▶ Leave the Tuff Spot for children to play with, but stay near so you can observe and give help if needed. Encourage the children to use the implements to cut and peel, exploring the flesh, skins and seeds of the fruit and vegetables. It's sometimes a good idea to fix a fork in the fruit or vegetable so it's easier for children to hold and cut.

Ideas for adult-initiated activities

▶ Join the children and talk about the different fruits and vegetables. Can they name the fruits and vegetables? Can they talk about similarities and differences in colour, shape, texture, smell, seeds in the different sorts you have offered?

▶ Look at the cut foods with magnifying glasses. Examine some of the seeds and pips, and photograph what the children have found.

▶ Talk about what the seeds are for and how you might be able to make them grow. Plant some!

▶ Discuss and record favourites in diagrams, photos or pictures. Write or record what children say about their favourites.

And another idea...

Make some food with fruit and vegetables (don't re-use ones the children have been playing with). Try making jam, fruit salad, soup, salsa or vegetable stew – some children will be amazed that food comes from real vegetables.

Google search: images – 'fruit' or 'vegetables'.

Incy wincy spider

Focus

Experiment with glue and glitter, then make wonderful webs for display.

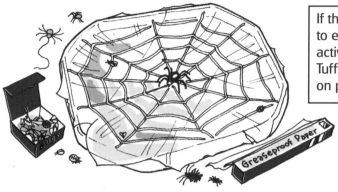

> If the children are going to eat food used for this activity, use a 'for food' Tuff Spot. See guidance on page 8.

What you need:

▶ PVA glue in squeezy bottle

▶ glitter (lots!)

▶ greaseproof paper

▶ plastic spiders

▶ cooking oil (optional)

▶ The story of 'The Very Busy Spider'

Contribution to Early Learning Goals

PRIME

Communication and language ① ② ③
Physical development ①
PSED ① ② ③

SPECIFIC

Knowledge of the world ① ②
Expressive arts and design ① ②

What you do:

This is a lovely activity to follow a walk on a damp, foggy or frosty day, or any day when you can see spider webs in the outdoor area.

1. Get a good supply of glitter – this activity needs plenty! It is also a good idea to put the Tuff Spot tray on a table so children can stand up to work.

2. Put the glitter in the Tuff Spot and let the children explore what it can do (you may need to protect the table or floor).

Independent exploration

▶   Let the children explore the glitter and talk about what it does, and how it can be used to decorate things.

Ideas for adult-initiated activities

▶   Collect the glitter together (a soft, decorating brush is best for this), and tip it all into a container for use later.

▶   Read the 'Very Busy Spider' story (or another spider story) together, and look carefully at the spiders' webs. Try drawing some on paper or whiteboards.

▶   Line the Tuff Spot with greaseproof paper and help the children to draw a big spider's web with felt pen. If you want the paper to be transparent when the web is finished, rub a little cooking oil gently all over the **back** of the paper before putting it in the Tuff Spot.

▶   Now help the children to draw lines of glue along each line of the web (small squeezy bottles make this easier).

▶   Sprinkle glitter all over the web and add a spider while the glue is wet.

▶   Leave to dry for several hours (or overnight), then lift the paper gently and tip the spare glitter off into the Tuff Spot. You should have a lovely sparkly spider's web to display in your setting.

▶   Display over a window or against a light for the best effect.

And another idea...

Let the children make their own webs on smaller pieces of greaseproof or black paper.

Explore spiders and their lives by looking at real spiders, books about spiders or searching information on the Internet.

Google search: images – 'spider web' or 'spider'.

Cold places

Focus

Explore ice and snow by constructing cold worlds in different places and with different materials.

What you need:

▶ ice cubes, lumps of ice, ice shapes

▶ cushion filling or 'instant snow'

▶ model boats

▶ small world animals (penguins, seals, polar bears and people)

Contribution to Early Learning Goals

PRIME

Communication and language ① ② ③
Physical development ①
PSED ① ② ③

SPECIFIC

Knowledge of the world ① ② ③
Expressive arts and design ① ②

What you do:

1. Look at some pictures together, either on a computer or in a book. Younger children might enjoy watching a Pingu story on TV.

2. This activity does need some preparation, but the children could help by filling containers of all sorts, sizes and shapes with water and putting them in a freezer (or outside on a very cold night!).

3. When frozen, put some of the ice shapes in a Tuff Spot and leave a basket of appropriate small world figures and some cushion filling for snow nearby.

Independent exploration

▶ Leave the Tuff Spot for children to play with, selecting play objects (polar bears, penguins, seals, Eskimo people, kayaks etc.). They could also add snow to their scenes by using man-made cushion filling.

Ideas for adult-initiated activities

▶ Share stories – a few about polar bears are: 'The Polar Bear and the Snow Cloud' by Jane Cabrira, 'A Boy and a Bear' by Lori Light, 'Little Polar Bear' by Hans de Beer – and talk about life in cold places.

▶ Put some ice cubes or shapes in the Tuff Spot and watch them melt. Adding some salt will speed up the process.

▶ Create some ice sculptures in rubber gloves, wellies or other unusual containers. Or freeze water in big containers such as ice cream tubs or small buckets, adding some food colouring to the water.

▶ Put some ice cubes in the Tuff Spot. Add some guttering or tubes and watch how the ice slides down the slopes.

▶ Make some flat ice sheets by freezing water in shallow trays or leaving the Tuff Spot full of water to freeze overnight. Experiment with your ice sheets, using toy cars and other vehicles, and talk about safety in freezing weather.

And another idea...

Freeze a variety of objects in ice cubes and larger pieces of ice (coins, crayons, sweets, buttons, petals, seeds, sequins and beads). Provide some small utensils and safety goggles so they can chip away at the ice to discover what is hidden inside. Were their predictions correct?

Google search: images – 'Eskimo', 'arctic', 'polar bear', 'sea ice' and 'penguin'.

Sugar igloo

Focus

Explore construction in a different environment and a different culture.

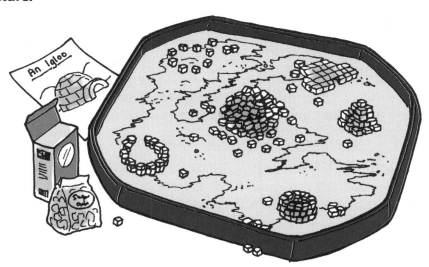

What you need:

▶ a box of sugar cubes

▶ a small amount of sugar

Contribution to Early Learning Goals

PRIME
Communication and language ① ② ③
Physical development ①
PSED ① ② ③

SPECIFIC
Knowledge of the world ① ②
Expressive arts and design ① ②

What you do:

1. This activity helps children to explore construction, balance and 3D shapes, as well as thinking about different sorts of homes and buildings in different environments.

2. As children play with bricks and mathematical cubes such as Unifix, talk with them about how the pieces fit together and how they can make stable structures with regular shapes.

3. Sprinkle sugar in the bottom of the Tuff Spot and leave the box of cubes in the middle.

Independent exploration

▶ Let the children explore the cubes, building and balancing them in the tray. If you are able to join them, talk about what they are doing and the ways they are building.

Ideas for adult-initiated activities

▶ Work with the children, making towers of different heights and thicknesses.

▶ Make a structure yourself and ask the children to copy what you have made.

▶ Look at a picture of an igloo and see how the igloo is made from cubes and cuboids of snow. Can the children make a house or other structure with the sugar cubes? Make a sugar cube home for a small world penguin or a polar bear. Read Arctic stories or watch Pingu DVDs.

▶ Talk about the sugar cubes and the loose sugar – what are they made of. How do you turn sugar into sugar cubes? Can you turn sugar cubes into sugar?

And another idea...

Count cubes in ones, twos and fives. Make patterns with the cubes, in lines, rows and steps.

Drop tiny drops of food colouring on sugar cubes - watch what happens.

Put cubes in tiny amounts of water in shallow trays and watch them gradually dissolve. Talk about dissolving sugar to sweeten drinks.

Dissolve some of the sugar in water, add colouring and use it to paint with. The paintings will dry to a nice shiny surface.

Paint watery paint on paper, then sprinkle icing sugar on it. Watch what happens.

Beach holiday

Focus

Make a miniature beach and recall holiday fun, by exploring a new small world.

What you need:

- ▶ sand and water
- ▶ small world figures and accessories
- ▶ materials to make boats, deck chairs etc.
- ▶ cocktail umbrellas

or

- ▶ shells, seaweed (real or from an aquarium shop)
- ▶ small world sea creatures
- ▶ little nets for fishing

I will need

Contribution to Early Learning Goals

PRIME

Communication and language ① ② ③
Physical development ①
PSED ① ② ③

SPECIFIC

Knowledge of the world ① ②
Expressive arts and design ① ②

What you do:

1. This activity is fun for indoors or outside, and will be more relevant in summer for most children, especially those who don't live near the sea. You could either make a seaside with play people, deck chairs and summer holidays, or a shoreline with shells, crabs, seaweed etc. You could set up the the Tuff Spot seaside after making a visit, or reading a story about the seaside.

2. It's probably a good idea to lift one side of the Tuff Spot tray slightly by wedging a stone or a folded towel under it, so the water stays at one end. Otherwise, the beach will just get wetter and wetter.

3. Let the children help you to put some damp sand in one end and some water in the lower end. Add some seaside accessories, people, objects, boats etc.

Independent exploration

▶ Leave the Tuff Spot for children to play with, using the seaside stimuli you have offered. Make sure they have plenty of time to explore the sand and the sea, telling stories and re-living experiences they may have had or heard about. Encourage them to add other objects such as shells and seaweed.

Ideas for adult-initiated activities

▶ Talk about going on holiday, what happens, how you get there, who else is there, what language is spoken, the weather etc.

▶ Make tiny boats to float on the sea, look at pictures of English seaside towns and talk about piers, promenades, breakwaters, donkey rides. Or look at some holiday brochures and make a foreign seaside with boats, paragliding, parasols and beach loungers.

▶ Use bags and small suitcases with holiday clothes for different sorts of holidays. Collect holiday clothes words.

And another idea...

Make signs and notices for the seaside, or take photos of the seaside you have made and print them on card to make postcards.

Set up a travel agent's in your setting, with brochures, tickets, passports, computer booking, posters etc. Or have a hotel in your role-play area with luggage, room keys, room service, swimming pool and children's play area.

Treasure hunt

Focus

Look for treasures of all sorts in sand, shavings, compost or other hidden places.

What you need:

▶ sand or other material to cover the 'treasure'

▶ a good collection of shiny stones, pebbles, glass or other beads

▶ sieves, brushes and small bowls

Contribution to Early Learning Goals

PRIME
Communication and language ① ② ③
Physical development ①
PSED ① ② ③

SPECIFIC
Knowledge of the world ① ②
Expressive arts and design ① ②

What you do:

1. Collect a good selection of 'treasure' for the children to sieve, sort and pick out of the Tuff Spot. Decide what you will use to cover the objects (this may affect the range and size of objects you use and the tools for retrieving them!).

2. Put the objects in the Tuff Spot and bury them with a good layer of whatever covering material you are using.

3. Leave some tools and small bowls beside the tray.

Independent exploration

▶ Talk to the children about being a treasure hunter and show them the tools they can use. Let them try to find the objects without using their fingers, just the tools – sieves, brushes, tongs, tweezers, spoons with holes etc. They can collect their treasure in individual bowls or yogurt pots.

Ideas for adult-initiated activities

▶ Sit with the children and talk about what they find – explore colours and shapes, count the objects, use 'more' and 'less' to compare what the children have collected. Use magnifying glasses so that the children can look closely at things.

▶ Talk about the different tools – using the correct names and comparing which are best for digging, for separating, for holding the objects.

▶ As the children get more adept at this activity, add some smaller objects – sequins, glitter, small beads, and discuss other tools that may be useful.

▶ Change the mixture – try porridge oats, rice, jelly, cooked pasta, compost or flour instead of sand.

And another idea...

Put the objects in water instead of sand and collect them in small aquarium nets.

Hide numbers and the same number of each object, so children have to collect whatever number they get first. Alternatively, bury letters with matching objects for each letter sound.

Offer white boards for recording what they find, or for making treasure maps.

Google search: images – 'treasure', 'archaeology', 'gold', 'jewels'.

Is it for me?

Focus

Send and receive notes, challenges, letters and messages through this new medium!

What you need:

- ▶ sand
- ▶ coloured and white paper
- ▶ envelopes (not essential)
- ▶ pencils
- ▶ pens

Contribution to Early Learning Goals

PRIME

Communication and language ① ② ③
Physical development ①
PSED ① ② ③

SPECIFIC

Literacy ① ②
Knowledge of the world ①
Expressive arts and design ① ②

What you do:

You will need to adapt this activity according to the age and ability of the children in your group. You may want to offer younger, less experienced children picture clues and things to find. Older, more experienced children will love having tiny letters to read and challenges to undertake.

1. You could read 'The Jolly Postman' as an introduction to the activity, or set up a post office in your role-play area.

2. Make some little letters (tiny envelopes would be lovely, but they aren't essential). Using tiny writing and small pieces of paper, you could write messages, ask questions, set challenges, draw pictures or cut pictures from catalogues. Fold the letters up and hide them in a Tuff Spot of dry sand (wet sand will cause problems!).

Independent exploration

▶ Leave the Tuff Spot for children to discover – you could tell them that a postman has dropped his bag and all the letters have got buried in the sand, or you could put a big letter or sign on top of the Tuff Spot saying that the postman needs some help.

▶ Sit with the children as they uncover and read the letters, helping them if they need it.

Ideas for adult-initiated activities

▶ Bury some more letters with specific challenges. These could include words to write, shapes to find, numbers to say or write, counting challenges – anything you want children to practise.

▶ Put individual children's names on the challenges so you can make them even more specific to their needs. One child pulls out a letter, reads the name and then the named child must do the challenge.

And another idea...

Use close-up photos of familiar objects in your setting for children to guess or find.

Get the children to write letters for each other. They could even write letters or challenges for friends in other classes or groups and invite them to visit to find out the answers.

Google search: images – 'treasure hunt', 'lucky dip'.

Soapy letters

Focus

Exploring mark–making and writing in a different medium.

Use a non-allergenic soap if you have any concerns about allergic reactions.

What you need:

▶ two or three bars of soap (good quality soap works best)
▶ brushes of different sizes and thicknesses
▶ warm water
▶ a foam decorating roller

I will need

Contribution to Early Learning Goals

PRIME
Communication and language ① ② ③
Physical development ①
PSED ① ② ③

SPECIFIC
Literacy ②
Knowledge of the world ① ②
Expressive arts and design ① ②

What you do:

1. Join the children when they wash their hands and talk about what soap is for and where the soap bubbles come from.

2. Put about an inch of warm water into the Tuff Spot and add a couple of bars of soap – you could cut the bars in half to make more pieces.

Independent exploration

▶ Show the children how to make a soapy lather by rubbing the soap bars in their hands. Add more warm water if they need it, but not too much!

▶ When they have a layer of soap suds, offer the children some brushes to make pictures, trails and marks in the foam with their fingers.

▶ Show them how to erase the marks with the decorating roller.

Ideas for adult-initiated activities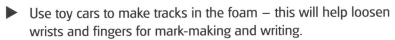

▶ Use toy cars to make tracks in the foam – this will help loosen wrists and fingers for mark-making and writing.

▶ Sit with the children and make patterns and regular marks yourself in the foam with your fingers or brushes – circles, zigzags, spirals, vertical and horizontal lines.

▶ You can use the foam to practise writing letters, names and other familiar words.

▶ Support confident mark-making by encouraging children to erase any marks they are not happy with, then have another go.

▶ Put a blob of ready mixed paint in one corner of the tray, and encourage the children to talk about what happens as they incorporate the paint into the foamy bubbles.

And another idea...

Hide some small objects in the foam and use brushes to tease them out, or use plastic tweezers.

Put some big buttons, glass beads or other obstacles in the tray and challenge the children to use a thin paint brush to negotiate a line in and out of the obstacles without touching them.

Google search: 'how does soap work?' or images of 'foam'.

Find the sound

Focus

Offer some sound practise with letters and objects by hiding letters and matching objects in shavings, shreddings or compost.

What you need:

- ▶ plastic letters
- ▶ small objects to match the letters
- ▶ shavings, straw or shredded paper
- ▶ whiteboard and pen, or chalkboard and chalk

Contribution to Early Learning Goals

PRIME

Communication and language ① ② ③
Physical development ①
PSED ① ② ③

SPECIFIC

Literacy ②
Mathematics ①
Expressive arts and design ① ②

What you do:

1. Spread some letters and objects out on a table and look at them with the children. See if they can pair them up – each object with its initial letter.

2. Mix the objects and letters up and scoop them into the Tuff Spot.

3. Cover them with a thick layer of straw, shavings or shredded paper.

Independent exploration

▶ Leave the Tuff Spot for children to explore – finding objects and their letters, and collecting them together till they have the whole set. You could provide some small bowls for individual collections or a big one to share. Or the children could lay the letters and objects out in matching pairs on a tray or board.

Ideas for adult-initiated activities

▶ Take turns to pull out a letter or object and say the initial sound. Now see who is the first to find the letter to match. To make this harder you could do this by touch alone.

▶ Limit the selection to consonants or vowels.

▶ Have more than one object for each letter.

▶ Have a small whiteboard or blackboard and record the letters as you find them. Start by doing the recording yourself, then let children write their own.

▶ Get the children to challenge each other by choosing objects and preparing the activity for others to complete.

▶ Organise pairs of children to help each other to play this game unaided as you observe their growing knowledge of letters and sounds.

▶ Just use letters, and children must say a word beginning or ending with that sound.

And another idea...

Extend the challenge by using middle or final sounds.

Make letters from salt and flour dough. Bake them, paint them with a mixture of paint and PVA glue, and hide them in the straw for finding.

Use wooden or plastic numbers and small objects for 'Find and Count' games.

Shoot

Focus

Aim at numbers with coloured water in a water pistol, and score if your aim is accurate.

What you need:

► water pistols
► water
► paint
► laminated numbers
► chalkboards or whiteboards
► more than one Tuff Spot

Contribution to Early Learning Goals

PRIME

Communication and language ① ② ③
Physical development ①
PSED ① ② ③

SPECIFIC

Literacy ②
Mathematics ①

What you do:

1. Make a set of laminated numbers (you could stick them on target shapes like this if you like).

2. Attach these in random order to the bottom of one or more Tuff Spots.

3. Take the Tuff Spots out into the garden and lean them up against a wall, tree, fence or climbing frame.

4. Draw a chalk line about 2 metres away. This is the shooting line.

5. Mix some water with paint in several colours. It should be thin and diluted, but the children still need to see which colour is which. Fill the water pistols with this mixture – a different colour for each.

Independent exploration

▶ The game is suitable for three or four children to every Tuff Spot, no more. Leave the children to explore the water and the water pistols.

Ideas for adult-initiated activities

▶ Discuss scoring, winning, losing. Help them with scoring their informal games on a blackboard or whiteboard.

▶ Call out numbers for them to aim at. Several children can fire at once – you will know who gets it right from the colour. Give a point for each strike, and keep score on a whiteboard.

▶ Older children could fire at numbers in turn from 1–5 or 1–10. Really bright mathematicians could fire at two numbers that make 10 or two numbers that make 8.

And another idea...

Try questions like 'Shoot at 1 less than 5,' 'Shoot at 5 add 2 more,' 'Shoot at a number bigger than 4' etc.

Stick up letters instead of numbers, and give children word or sound challenges such as 'The letter at the beginning of 'mushroom', 'The letter at the end of 'boat'.

Fishy numbers

Focus

A new version of a traditional favourite – a number fishing activity and simple experiment in magnetism.

What you need:

- ▶ water
- ▶ paper clips
- ▶ numbered and laminated cardboard fish
- ▶ sticks, string and small magnets
- ▶ small buckets or bowls

Contribution to Early Learning Goals

PRIME

Communication and language ① ② ③

Physical development ① ②

PSED ① ② ③

SPECIFIC

Mathematics ①

What you do:

1. Let the children help to make some fish from thin card, colour them with felt pens and add a number of dots from 1 – 5 to each fish (you can have duplicates). Laminate the fish.

2. Attach a paper clip to each fish.

3. Make some fishing rods by tying string to the magnets and fixing these onto the sticks.

Independent exploration

▶ Put some water in the Tuff Spot, add the fish and leave the children to take turns fishing with the rods. Each child puts their catch in their own bucket or bowl.

Ideas for adult-initiated activities

▶ Children must recognise the number and say it, or else the fish goesback in the pond.

▶ When a child has caught two fish they must tell you the total score.

▶ Children practise writing numbers by putting their own scores on a black or whiteboard.

▶ Make some more fish for the game. Put numbers on these fish and children could just catch one fish, naming the number or the amount of dots.

▶ Children could also try to catch pairs of fish, one with dots and the other with numbers.

▶ Make fish with high frequency words for the children to recognise as they catch the fish.

And another idea...

Play the game indoors – children will still enjoy fishing without water! Just put the fish in a dry Tuff Spot and play again.

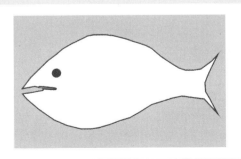

Sticky spaghetti

Focus
Sticky spaghetti is great for all sorts of activities. It doesn't need glue!

What you need:

▶ spaghetti – cooked, drained and cooled
▶ knives, spoons, spatulas
▶ tweezers
▶ black paper
▶ plastic numbers

I will need

Contribution to Early Learning Goals

PRIME
Communication and language ① ② ③
Physical development ①
PSED ① ② ③

SPECIFIC
Literacy ②
Mathematics ①
Knowledge of the world ②
Expressive arts and design ① ②

What you do:

1. When cooked, spaghetti releases a lot of starch which will stick it to a surface.

2. Cook the spaghetti in plenty of water. Leave it to cool.

3. Tip the spaghetti into the Tuff Spot.

Independent exploration

▶ Leave the some tools and utensils in or near the Tuff Spot for child-initiated play.

Ideas for adult-initiated activities

▶ If they have not already discovered this, show the children how they can make shapes with the spaghetti. Challenge them to make circles, straight lines, wiggles and other patterns.

▶ Now see if you can make letters and numbers together. Show them how they can cut spaghetti strands into shorter lengths when they need to.

▶ Just use tweezers to lift single strands of spaghetti out of the Tuff Spot tray.

▶ Challenge the children to make a letter or number when you say it. Talk about why it is easier to make curvy numbers and letters.

▶ Give the children a sheet of black paper each and make letters and pictures on the paper with the spaghetti – it should stick to the paper if you make sure the pasta is damped down regularly (a hand spray is good for this).

▶ Line the whole Tuff Spot with black paper and make a big picture or a letter/number pattern all together. Hang the picture up when it is dry and talk about why you didn't need any glue.

▶ Use pasta (cooked and dry) in the Tuff Spot for sorting and counting as well as for free play with scoops, bags, spoons, scales, etc.

And another idea...

Try black cooked spaghetti with small world insects hidden in it! Children could remove the insects with tweezers. This gives a really good hand control practise.

Use smaller pasta shapes such as stars or alphabetti spaghetti for a change.

Down in the jungle

Focus

Make your own jungle and go exploring or on a small world safari.

What you need:

▶ house plants

▶ pebbles, grass, soil, sand and twigs

▶ hanging basket moss

▶ small world people and jungle animals

▶ a shallow tray

I will need

Contribution to Early Learning Goals

PRIME

Communication and language ① ② ③

Physical development ①

PSED ① ② ③

SPECIFIC

Knowledge of the world ① ②

Expressive arts and design ① ②

What you do:

1. Look at some books, film or DVDs before and during this activity. You could try 'Rumble in the Jungle', 'Elmer', 'The Jungle Book' or a 'Planet Earth' DVD.

2. Line the Tuff Spot with grass or moss, and create a clearing with sand.

3. Let the children help you to make the jungle by adding trees, twigs, stones and rocks, water in a tin lid, animals, people etc.

Independent exploration

▶ Leave the Tuff Spot jungle for children to play with, watching them as they work and taking some photos of the play as it develops.

▶ You could offer the children some hats and bags to wear as they play at jungles in the tray.

Ideas for adult-initiated activities

▶ Ask the children how you could make the jungle even more interesting – perhaps by hanging crêpe paper creepers from the ceiling, adding a painted background, putting some house plats round the Tuff Spot, or using their own ideas. Help them to research what they need. Make clay or dough animals for your scene.

▶ Talk about the river or pool you have made. use a magnifying glass to make the scene look more realistic. Talk about what the animals need. Take some photos and enlarge them to make a background.

▶ Talk about the animals that live in the jungle and those that live in desert, grassland, forest or mountain areas. Use books and the Internet to find out which animal lives where. Talk about what they eat, how they live and how their bodies and behaviour protect them in their chosen habitat. Move like animals to jungle music!

And another idea...

Think about the sounds of the jungle and see if you can make a tape recording of your own jungle music to play in the background.

Go on a 'Jungle Safari' wearing suitable hats and camouflage clothes. Make lists of what you need and the animals and plants you saw. Use the framework of 'The Bear Hunt' or 'Daddy's taking us to the zoo' to make a new song about going to the jungle.

Google Search: images – 'jungle animal', 'mountain animal', 'forest animal'.

A spot of gardening

Focus

Growing seeds and plants is always fascinating and rewarding. Use your Tuff Spot for a gardening experience.

What you need:

▶ trowels or old tablespoons

▶ plant pots, seeds

▶ compost

▶ a watering can

▶ sticky labels and pens

Contribution to Early Learning Goals

PRIME

Communication and language ① ② ③
Physical development ①
PSED ① ② ③

SPECIFIC

Literacy ②
Mathematics ①
Knowledge of the world ②
Expressive arts and design ① ②

What you do:

1. Collect some plants and seeds. Seeds are cheap and you get a lot for your money (try mustard and cress, beans, peas, or grass seed). Parents may have plants and seedlings that you can have for free.

2. Get some real, small-size tools, specially made for children.

3. You can get a lot of compost from a Growbag!

4. Fill the Tuff Spot with compost and leave the other things nearby. You will need to stay with this activity, especially when involving younger children or those with less control.

Independent exploration

▶ Leave the some tools and utensils in or near the Tuff Spot for child-initiated play.

Ideas for adult-initiated activities

▶ Show children different sorts of seeds and discuss what they grow into. Talk about what plants need to stay healthy. You could do some simple experiments with fast growing plants, putting some of them in the dark, leaving some without water, leaving some without soil. Look at the seeds every few days and record what happens by taking photos or drawing their progress.

▶ Try different places for growing seeds and plants – on the radiator, under a table, on a windowsill, in the sink, in different places outside. Put a basket of tools and seeds outside and suggest that children may like to plant some seeds direct into the soil.

▶ Go on a seed spotting walk – you should be able to find seeds in all seasons except deep snow or after severe frosts. Collect some of these seeds and plant them.

And another idea...

When you have fruit or vegetables for snack, collect the seeds and plant them – you will be surprised what you get!

Buy a watermelon, marrow, pomegranate or avocado pear and try growing their seeds. Cut seed potatoes into pieces and plant them, or grow carrot tops, or beans in jars.

Make labels, seed packets or chart the growth of what you plant.

Snail observatory

Focus

A fascinating but slow observation! Collect snails and watch them in your snail home.

What you need:

▶ snails
▶ water
▶ logs, leaves, twigs, soil and rocks
▶ lettuce leaves
▶ magnifying glasses

Contribution to Early Learning Goals

PRIME
Communication and language ① ② ③
Physical development ①
PSED ① ② ③

SPECIFIC
Knowledge of the world ②
Expressive arts and design ① ②

What you do:

1. Children love looking for and collecting snails. A damp day will be a good time. Look under stones, behind things and in dead leaves. If you don't find any, leave a few plant pots on their sides and cover these with some paper or plastic – this should tempt them.

2. Let the children help you to collect stones, twigs, sticks, logs etc. for your snail tray.

3. Put some damp soil in a Tuff Spot and let the children arrange the logs stones, etc. Add some dry leaves and a couple of lettuce leaves for food. Snails will be more lively if they are wet, so make sure they don't dry out.

Warning! Find a sheet of plastic or fabric to cover the snail house at night. Otherwise the snails will escape and eat things!

Independent exploration

▶ Let the children add the snails they have collected, and they will have a great time watching them explore their new home.

▶ Offer some magnifying glasses and a camera.

Ideas for adult-initiated activities

▶ Watch the snails together, talking about how they move and what they like to eat.

▶ Gently put some snails on black paper and watch them make silver trails as they move.

▶ Put some snails on a whole lettuce and see if you can hear them eating. Use a magnifying glass to see how they eat, how they move, how their eyes work. Watch what happens when they retract and extend their eyes, and what happens as they go into their shells.

▶ Get a piece of glass or perspex, and cover the edges with carpet or duct tape to make them safe. Gently lift some snails onto the glass and then look at the other side of the glass – you will be able to see how they move and how their mouths work.

And another idea...

Look at other animals that live in shells. Explore the spirals of their shells. Draw and paint spiral patterns.

A special day

Focus

Celebrate your own or someone else's birthday by making or decorating cakes.

If the children are going to eat food used for this activity, use a 'for food' Tuff Spot. See guidance on page 8.

What you need:

▶ cornflour
▶ water
▶ boiling water
▶ gelatin (or substitute)
▶ icing syringe
▶ decorations and plastic letters

Contribution to Early Learning Goals

PRIME
Communication and language ① ② ③
Physical development ①
PSED ① ② ③

SPECIFIC
Knowledge of the world ①
Expressive arts and design ① ②

What you do:

1. This activity starts with a big quantity of 'cake' mixture for decorating play. It is **not** for eating! See the 'And another idea...' box for edible versions.

2. To make the 'cake' mix 2 cups of corn flour with a cup of cold water to make a smooth paste. Add 4 cups of boiling water (adult only) and stir. Cook over a medium heat till the mixture thickens. Dissolve the gelatin in some warm water and add to the corn flour mixture. Mix well and leave to cool. It should be stiff but not solid.

Independent exploration

▶ Let the children help you to tip the 'cake mixture' into the Tuff Spot and spread it out with their hands or spoons.

▶ Offer some coloured, runnier corn flour mixture in icing syringes.

▶ Beads, sequins, plastic letters, glitter, candles and candle holders all make the big birthday cake activity more fun!

Ideas for adult-initiated activities

▶ Take some photos of the big cake activity and talk about the different ways groups of children decorated them.

▶ Talk about different sorts of cakes for different celebrations. If you can go to visit a bakery or supermarket, you could collect some more ideas.

▶ Make different mixes for big cakes – try salt dough, pastry or jelly.

▶ Help the children to make some salt and flour dough and work with them to make cakes, buns and biscuits. Bake these in a low oven, paint them and then set up a 'baker's shop'.

And another idea...

Buy some plain biscuits or fairy cakes to decorate with icing tubes and other edible decorations. Show the children the different sorts of decorations, and give them paper and felt pens to plan their design before they do the real thing.

Discuss the plans as they decorate the biscuits and cakes, and photograph them before they are eaten.

Now have a party with invitations, games and other treats.

Google search: 'birthday cake', or buy a kids' birthday cake book.

Cement mixer

Focus

Mix, pour and build – and be Bob the Builder for real!

What you need:

▶ sand
▶ water
▶ buckets and containers
▶ trowels and spades
▶ real bricks

Contribution to Early Learning Goals

PRIME
Communication and language ① ② ③
Physical development ①
PSED ① ② ③

SPECIFIC
Knowledge of the world ① ②
Expressive arts and design ① ②

What you do:

1. This activity uses real bricks and a sand-and-water mortar (real cement is not a good idea for small children). It is probably best done outside.

2. Try to get some small building or garden trowels. These will be much easier for children to handle.

3. Show the children how to mix 'mortar' in a bucket (roughly 1 scoop of sand to 1 scoop of water).

4. Put the bricks and tools near the Tuff Spot.

Independent exploration

▶ Let the children explore building with the real bricks and 'mortar'. Offer the camera so they can photograph their creations.

Ideas for adult-initiated activities

▶ Look at the photos they have taken of their work. Discuss the best way of building, and why some structures are stronger than others.

▶ Look at some images from Google or other searches. Alternatively, get some books about building.

▶ Go on a walk around your setting or your area and look for brick walls and their structures. Take some photos of different sorts and patterns of walls and buildings. Talk about windows, doors and other features of buildings.

▶ Challenge the children to make walls of a particular height or length.

▶ Use Lego or other unit construction sets to build walls and other structures. Work alongside the children and talk about what works best and why.

▶ Try making your own small building bricks with clay. Use a self-hardening sort so you don't have to fire them. If you are in a clay soil area, dig some clay yourselves to make genuine bricks.

And another idea...

Make word walls, picture walls and other sorts of displays with units.
Use a rectangular sponge to make brick prints on big pieces of paper. Use these as backing paper for a display of your work and photos, or to cover a book of photos and drawings.
Google search: 'builder' or 'bricklayer'.

Lotions and potions

Focus

Try these different ways of mixing face paint, skin lotion or finger paint.

Check for skin allergies before using face paints and other mixtures on skin.

What you need:

▶ lollipop sticks, spoons

▶ small empty plastic pots

▶ labels and pens

▶ toothpaste, food colouring, aromatherapy oils and water

▶ baby lotion/moisturiser

Contribution to Early Learning Goals

PRIME
Communication and language ① ② ③
Physical development ①
PSED ① ② ③

SPECIFIC
Literacy ① ②
Knowledge of the world ②
Expressive arts and design ① ②

What you do:

1. Children will want to try their lotions and potions, so make sure they understand they are **not** for eating, and must be used with care, only on exposed skin. Check for skin allergies.

2. Use baby lotion or unperfumed moisturiser as a base for these creams, then you can safely use them as face paints, or as your own moisturisers or creams.

3. Tip the moisturiser or baby lotion into small bowls. Arrange these and the other objects near the Tuff Spot. You may need to model the activity for younger children, showing them how to mix some moisturiser with colouring, water, perfumes etc. in a small container.

Independent exploration

▶ Encourage the children to mix and stir, scoop and pour until they are happy with their mixtures. Then offer labels so they can name their own bottles and jars.

Ideas for adult-initiated activities

▶ Talk about the different lotions and what they are for. Look at pictures of the body and discuss where you might need a lotion or cream.

▶ Make some face paints together, using moisturiser and food colouring. Provide a mirror for exploring face paints on themselves or each other. Younger children will enjoy putting face paints on dolls.

▶ Talk about why and when we use creams and lotions – sunscreen, baby lotion, dry skin, bites, minor injuries etc.

▶ Try mixing herbs and spices in lotions – lavender, mint, coriander or rosemary. Alternatively, use food flavourings such as orange oil or peppermint.

▶ Make up special names for the lotions – 'Lovely Lavender', 'Pretty Pink' or 'Peppermint Potion'.

▶ Collect the complimentary bottles from hotel bathrooms. Even the empty bottles are useful!

And another idea...

Set up your role-play area as a beauty salon, make-up shop or hospital. Set up shelves and trolleys of creams, bandages and other equipment. Let the children use their own mixtures to treat dolls or each other.

Google search: images – 'perfume bottle', 'moisturiser' or 'lotion.

You smell nice!

Focus

A new version of the rose petal perfume most adults made when they were children!

Check for allergies when using essential oils.

What you need:

▶ a selection of pots and bottles (camera film cases, hotel shampoo bottles)

▶ water

▶ food colouring

▶ aromatherapy oils (several different sorts)

Contribution to Early Learning Goals

PRIME

Communication and language ① ② ③
Physical development ①
PSED ① ② ③

SPECIFIC

Literacy ① ②
Mathematics ①
Knowledge of the world ②
Expressive arts and design ① ②

What you do:

1. Offer some foods for snack and experiences at other times that emphasise smells and scents. Oranges, hot chocolate, porridge, coffee, peppermint, perfumed candles, room sprays, pot pourri, and many more things have smells that are pleasant and evocative for both children and adults.

2. When you are outside, during cooking sessions or before lunch, draw children's attention to smells in the air or smells of materials they use.

3. Take a walk in your local area or in a supermarket or local shop, and smell the different places in your community – a grocer, a baker, a place of worship, a chemist's shop, a florist or greengrocer.

4. Put the bottle and jars, some jugs of water, aromatherapy oils and the pots and bottles in the Tuff Spot.

Independent exploration

▶ Leave the Tuff Spot for children to play with and experiment, but sit nearby so you can join the play and keep an eye on what happens.

Ideas for adult-initiated activities

▶ Make some perfumes together and label the bottles with suitable names and descriptions.

▶ Experiment together with oils and colours, talking about which perfumes go best with which colours and which names.

▶ Add some herbs, spices and other natural ingredients to the oils and perfumes – try star anise, lavender or peppermint oil.

▶ Set up a perfumery in your role-play area, with gift wrapping, trial bottles, samples, special offers etc. You could combine this activity with 'Lotions and potions' on the previous page, and offer creams and lotions as well.

▶ Use the role-play as a group activity. Sit with the children and make labels, lists, notices, signs for the perfumery, and use a till or credit card to extend the work into mathematical areas.

And another idea...

Ask friends, other staff, parents and carers to send in empty perfume bottles and packaging for the shop. This is particularly successful just after Christmas! If you need to keep them, collapse the packaging to store flat.

Google search: images – 'perfume bottle' or 'perfume packaging', recipes – making perfume'.

Fruit juice factory

Focus

Making your own juice is much more fun than buying it in a box.

If the children are going to eat food used for this activity, use a 'for food' Tuff Spot. See guidance on page 8.

What you need:

- ▶ lemons and oranges
- ▶ water
- ▶ small plastic bottles
- ▶ funnels, jugs and spoons
- ▶ sticky labels
- ▶ fruit squeezers

I will need

Contribution to Early Learning Goals

PRIME
Communication and language ① ② ③
Physical development ①
PSED ① ② ③

SPECIFIC
Literacy ②
Mathematics ① ②
Knowledge of the world ②
Expressive arts and design ① ②

What you do:

1. Make sure the Tuff Spot is clean, then let the children explore the equipment for a bit – see below.

Independent exploration

▶ At first, just offer the bottles, the funnels and jugs of water for free play. Children may need help with the equipment at first, and will need to practise managing the funnels and small bottles. Encourage them to be as independent as possible. If you find it difficult not to interfere, do an observation or take some photos about what happens.

Ideas for adult-initiated activities

▶ When the children have had time to practise using the equipment, you can start juicing!

▶ Halve some lemons and oranges and put them in the tray with the jugs of water and the other equipment.

▶ Explain to the children that they need a bottle, a funnel and a jug each. This will help to control the numbers!

▶ Show the children how to use the squeezers. They may find this difficult at first.

▶ Now help them to squeeze some juice, add some water to it, then pour it into their bottle. Let the children use the sticky labels to label their bottles – 'lemon', 'orange', or 'orange and lemon'.

▶ Go shopping and look at all the different sorts of juice on sale. If you can, buy some different sorts to taste and choose favourites. You could make a chart of favourite juices.

▶ Try some vegetable juices as well – tomato, carrot, beetroot.

And another idea...

Have juice instead of (or as well as) fruit at snack time. Make a juice bar in your setting, where children can choose which juice they have. Provide small plastic glasses or disposable cups and a couple of café tables and chairs. This may make a big difference to tastes and willingness to try new things.

Moon landing

Focus

Go exploring in this homemade moonscape.

What you need:

- ▶ shaving foam
- ▶ kitchen roll tubes and other recycled materials
- ▶ paper, paint, glue
- ▶ small world space people and equipment
- ▶ building bricks

Contribution to Early Learning Goals

PRIME
Communication and language ① ② ③
Physical development ①
PSED ① ② ③

SPECIFIC
Knowledge of the world ① ②
Expressive arts and design ① ②

What you do:

1. You could use this activity to follow up an interest among children, to follow a story or as part of a project or topic on transport or space.

2. Spend some time collecting the right sort of recycled materials for this activity – cardboard tubes, shapes for nose cones, lids and boxes for moon buggies, wheels, buttons etc.

3. If you have two Tuff Spots, you could use one for building and one for the moonscape. The moonscape could have a thick covering of shaving foam or fake snow.

Independent exploration

▶ Be available when the children are making their models of buggies, rockets, space stations etc. Offer books and other reference materials to help them with designs.

▶ When the children have made their models, suggest that they could use them to play on the 'moon'. Foam is great stuff for play and encourages language in a play situation.

Ideas for adult-initiated activities

▶ Look at books or pictures of the moon landings, and discuss what it would be like to be on the moon. Collect words and phrases that children use, and turn these into a moon poem or song, with some suitably space-themed music.

▶ Make up space stories together, or turn the role play area into a space station, a rocket, or a control centre.

▶ Make moon and space mobiles from card or use photos of the children's constructions.

▶ Enlarge some pictures of the children's work to use as a background for display or further play.

And another idea...

Make a space museum in the role play area, complete with labelled rockets and spaceships, space figures, moonscapes. Have a souvenir shop with all sorts of souvenirs – postcards made from your own photos, models, bookmarks, fact sheets, decorated paper plates and cups, telescopes and books.

Google search: 'moon', or 'space pictures'.

Alien planet

Focus

Move on from the moon and explore an alien land, complete with volcanoes, monsters and other adventures in space.

What you need:

- ► play dough (big quantities)
- ► rolling pins and other modelling tools
- ► tissue paper and paper shreddings

Contribution to Early Learning Goals

PRIME

Communication and language ① ② ③
Physical development ①
PSED ① ② ③

SPECIFIC

Mathematics ①
Knowledge of the world ① ②
Expressive arts and design ① ②

What you do:

1. Let the children help you make some dough.

Independent exploration

▶ Tip the dough into the Tuff Spot and help the children to roll it out.

▶ Now help the children to shape the surface into hills, lumps, craters and other shapes. You could put some crumpled newspaper under some places to make hills.

▶ Now let the children make aliens from plasticene or make some more dough and colour it strange colours.

Ideas for adult-initiated activities

▶ If you want a more permanent surface, try covering your dough landscape with sheets of paper which the children have painted with wallpaper paste. If you layer the surface with several sheets, then let it dry, you will have a hard surface that can be painted and decorated with trees, moss, stones, gravel, foil and other materials.

▶ Use the landscape for story telling and imaginative work.

▶ Collect some words and use these to make an alien chant or song, then sing this as you play.

▶ You could take turns giving each other instructions, such as 'Drive the alien buggy under the green tree', 'Put the blue alien in the hole under the tree', 'If you climb the purple hill, what can you see?'

And another idea...

Make up an alien language together. Children love this because anything goes and they can't get it wrong, even when they write messages!

Use a camera or a video camera to make a book or a film of the stories you tell with the aliens.

Wonderful wellies

Focus

Step out in your wellies and create a work of art!

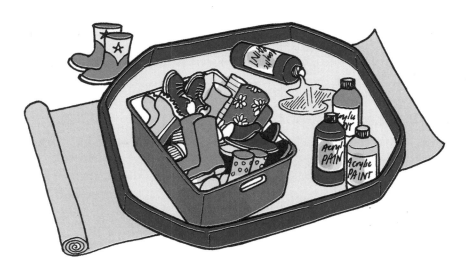

What you need:

▶ wellingtons and outdoor shoes with patterns on their soles

▶ paint in different colours

▶ rolls of paper

Contribution to Early Learning Goals

PRIME

Communication and language ① ② ③

Physical development ①

PSED ① ② ③

SPECIFIC

Knowledge of the world ②

Expressive arts and design ① ②

What you do:

1. When you take children outside on wet or muddy days, look at the patterns their boots and shoes make in mud, water or snow.

2. Collect a range of suitable shoes and boots. You could try the lost property box, ask parents or even try charity shops, car boot sales or rummage sales for unusual ones.

3. Take the Tuff Spot outside and let the children choose the first colour. Tip this into the Tuff Spot.

4. Roll the paper out, securing one end under the Tuff Spot and the other end with some big bricks or stones.

5. A hose or bucket of water would be useful!

Independent exploration

▶ Let the children choose which footwear to put on, then help them to walk through the paint and along the paper.

Ideas for adult-initiated activities

▶ Talk about all the different ways you could move along the paper – hopping, jumping with feet together, skipping, striding, even walking backwards. Experiment with some of these.

▶ Put half the pairs of shoes at one end of the paper and half at the other, and let the children walk in one pair down the paper and another on the way back.

▶ Put the right shoe from each pair in a pile at one end of the paper, and the left shoes in a pile at the other end. Help the children to hop through the paint, hop down the paper, find the other shoe and walk or jump back.

▶ Try with different shoes on each foot, or with two left boots or two right ones.

▶ Choose a friend and walk, jump or hop down the paper holding hands. Alternatively, walk 'three legged' by tying your right leg to your friend's left leg.

And another idea...

Customise your footwear by attaching things to make the prints different.

Attach string around the boots/shoes and tie at the top to make a stripy print, or cut out foam shapes and glue them to the bottom of the shoe.

Google search: 'footprints', 'shoes', 'boots'.

Porridge play

Focus

Goldilocks never had time to explore the porridge, but your children can! There are several ways to do this.

If the children are going to eat food used for this activity, use a 'for food' Tuff Spot. See guidance on page 8.

What you need:

- porridge oats
- spoons, bowls and water
- jam, sugar and golden syrup
- sultanas and currants
- fruit such as blueberries, raspberries and stewed apples

Contribution to Early Learning Goals

PRIME
Communication and language ① ② ③
Physical development ①
PSED ① ② ③

SPECIFIC
Mathematics ① ②
Knowledge of the world ① ②
Expressive arts and design ① ②

What you do:

1. Read or tell the story of 'The Three Bears', then let the children act it out as you retell the story again.

2. Tip a small amount of porridge oats into a bowl and talk together about what it looks, feels, smells and tastes like.

3. Make some porridge together. Talk about how the porridge oats change as they cook. Let the children choose how they would like to eat their own small bowl of porridge. Children will often be prepared to taste things when they are with their friends.

4. Either tip the remaining porridge (without additions) into the Tuff Spot, or if it has all been eaten make some more.

Independent exploration

▶ Offer a basket of tools and utensils for play with the porridge. Collect spoons forks, ladles, cups, yogurt pots, small pans etc. Offer some things in three different sizes to continue 'The Three Bears' theme.

▶ Watch and listen to what the children do and say.

Ideas for adult-initiated activities

▶ Talk about favourite flavours for the porridge and use the information to make a chart or graph.

▶ Change the experience by putting a whole pile of dry porridge oats in the Tuff Spot. Talk about the difference in texture, colour and smell between the two.

▶ Use porridge making to explore instructions and sequences. Take a series of photos for a sequencing discussion or a game.

▶ Talk about breakfast, the importance of having something to eat before they leave home, and how this helps them to think, learn and play. Discuss favourite breakfasts, and the differences between what people eat on weekdays and what they eat at the weekend when they have more time.

And another idea...

Turn your role-play area into the Three Bears' house.

Put runny cooked porridge in the Tuff Spot for play with diggers and trucks. Children can make tracks with wheels, load up porridge, pile it up, and tip it out.

Google Search: 'porridge', 'Three Bears', 'breakfast'.

Bread maker and sculptor

Focus

Make bread, bake bread and build sculptures!

If the children are going to eat food used for this activity, use a 'for food' Tuff Spot. See guidance on page 8.

What you need:

- ▶ two Tuff Spots
- ▶ scales, flour and water for free play
- ▶ ready-mixed bread mix for bread making
- ▶ milk
- ▶ aprons, spoons, bowls and baking sheets

Contribution to Early Learning Goals

PRIME

Communication and language ① ② ③
Physical development ①
PSED ① ② ③

SPECIFIC

Mathematics ① ②
Knowledge of the world ②
Expressive arts and design ① ②

What you do:

1. This activity provides free play with flour and water and a chance to make some bread to eat.

2. Look at the flour together and talk about how it looks, feels, smells, even how it tastes. Talk about where flour comes from. Look at some books about harvests and bread making.

3. Tip a good pile of flour in the Tuff Spot and offer a jug of water.

Independent exploration

▶ Leave the Tuff Spot for children to play with, adding water if they want to, and making different consistencies of dough. Make sure they have some extra flour available to thicken up the mixture when it gets too wet!

Ideas for adult-initiated activities

▶ Use the clean Tuff Spot (or a bowl) to make some bread from a bread mix. Look at the ingredients on the bag or box, so children know that you need more ingredients than just flour to make bread.

▶ Follow the instructions on the bag as you help the children to make the bread. Then give each child a small amount of dough to shape, twist, pound and roll.

▶ Put the bread shapes on a baking tray, brush the tops with a little milk, and bake them according to the instructions.

▶ When the bread is baked, enjoy eating it together with butter and cheese or jam.

▶ As you eat, read the story of 'The Little Red Hen', or sing 'Pat-a-Cake' or 'Five Brown Rolls at the Baker's Shop'.

And another idea...

Make some flour and salt dough and use this to make sculptures. This dough makes lovely decorations for Christmas or other festivals. Make 3D shapes, or use cutters to make shapes and figures. Make patterns on these using a stick or small fork, then make a hole right through to hang them up. Bake on a low heat until hard, then paint them or leave them natural colour. Seal them with varnish or PVA glue and thread a ribbon or string through the hole. As another activity, you could make fruit, vegetables, cakes, burgers or pizzas for shops, take-aways and other role-play situations.

Google search: 'bread', 'bread sculpture' or 'salt dough recipe'.

Fishy exploration

Focus

You may not enjoy this, but the children will be fascinated! Just do as much as you feel comfortable with.

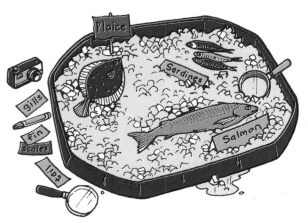

If the children are going to eat food used for this activity, use a 'for food' Tuff Spot. See guidance on page 8.

What you need:

- ▶ one or more fresh, whole fish
- ▶ a bag of ice (from a supermarket or freezer)
- ▶ magnifying glasses
- ▶ a sharp knife (adult only)

Contribution to Early Learning Goals

PRIME
Communication and language ① ② ③
Physical development ①
PSED ① ② ③

SPECIFIC
Literacy ① ②
Knowledge of the world ① ②
Expressive arts and design ① ②

What you do:

1. This activity gives a good opportunity to take a group on a shopping trip to your local supermarket or fish market.

2. Buy a fish or two. Get whole fish, not fillets – the experience will be much better. Choose cheaper fish such as mackerel or herrings, or smaller fish such as whitebait or sprats.

3. Look at everything and take some photos of other fish.

4. Buy a bag of ice if you haven't got any in your setting.

5. When you get back to your setting, tip some ice into the Tuff Spot and put the fish in too. The ice will keep the fish fresh for longer!

Independent exploration

▶ Let the children explore the fish you have bought, looking at the scales, mouths, teeth, fins etc.

▶ Sit with them as they explore, answering questions and modelling the words they need to describe the parts of the fish.

Ideas for adult-initiated activities

▶ Take one of the fish and talk in detail about its features – the colour, shape, texture of skin and scales, the fins and tail. Hold the fish in your hands and move it as if it were swimming. Try gently stretching out the fins and talking about what they are for and how they work to help with swimming and balance.

▶ Look at the fish closely through magnifying glasses, looking at scales, teeth etc.

▶ Gently open the fishes mouths and look at their tongues and teeth. Look at their gills – how do they help the fish to breathe under water? Look at their eyes – are they like human eyes?

▶ Try cutting the fish open down its stomach and looking at the inside – what can you see? Can you see its bones? ...its stomach? ...its muscles?

And another idea...

Try making fish prints (Gyotaku in Japanese). Wipe the fish with kitchen roll and salt to remove any oils. Paint the fish on one side – don't paint the eye.

Press some paper or thin fabric over the painted fish and carefully peel it off again to get a fish print. (Don't eat fish that have been painted!)

Google search: 'fish', 'fishing boats', 'fishermen' or 'fish and chips'!

Fairy cake recipe

Makes 12 fairy cakes. Linked to 'A special day' on page 46.

What you need:

▶ 85g softened butter

▶ 85g caster sugar

▶ 1 large egg

▶ 140g self-raising flour

What you do:

1. Preheat the oven to 200°C/gas mark 6.

2. Arrange 12 paper cake cases on a baking tray or bun tin.

3. Beat the butter and sugar together until pale and fluffy.

4. Beat in the egg.

5. Sift the flour and salt into a bowl, and using a metal spoon, quickly fold the flour into the butter mixture.

6. Spoon the mixture into the paper cases.

7. Bake for 15 minutes until they are well-risen and golden. If you press a cake lightly, the sponge should bounce back.

8. Cool on a wire rack.

9. Decorate as you wish!

Letter match objects

Most of these objects are easy to get hold of – look in your small world/role-play equipment. Alternatively, you could print and laminate pictures of the more elusive items.

A – ant, apple.
B – bib, bed, book, brush, button, banana, ball.
C – card, carrot, car, crab, carpet, crayon, candle, cup, coin, cow.
D – dog, dice, dinosaur, doll.
E – egg, envelope, elephant.
F – fork, four, five, foil, frog, fish.
G – glasses, glue, goat.
H – horse, harmonica, house.
I – igloo, ink.
J – jigsaw piece, jug, jewel.
K – key, king.
L – lid, letter, leaf, laces, lollipop, Lego, lemon.
M – marble, match, man, mouse.
N – nine, nose, nail.
O – orange, octopus.
P – picture, paper, pig, plate, pencil, penny, peg, pen.
Q – quaver, queen.
R – ring, rubber, ruler.
S – spoon, six, seven, sun, star, sock, scissors, spider.
T – two, ten, tissue, tiger.
U – umbrella.
V – violin.
W – wood, window.
X – x-ray.
Y – yoyo, yacht.
Z – zebra.
Th – three, thimble, thirty.
Ch – church, cheese, cherry.
Sh – shoe, shark, sharpener, sheep.

If you have found this book useful you might also like ...

LB Making Poetry
ISBN 978-1-4081-1250-2

LB Christmas
ISBN 978-1-9022-3364-2

LB Discovery Bottles
ISBN 978-1-9060-2971-5

LB Music
ISBN 978-1-9041-8754-7

All available from
www.bloomsbury.com/featherstone

The Little Books Club

There is always something in Little Books to help and inspire you. Packed full of lovely ideas, Little Books meet the need for exciting and practical activities that are fun to do, address the Early Learning Goals and can be followed in most settings. Everyone is a winner!

We publish 5 new Little Books a year. Little Books Club members receive each of these 5 books as soon as they are published for a reduced price. The subscription cost is £29.99 – a one off payment that buys the 5 new books for £4.99 instead of £8.99 each.

In addition to this, Little Books Club Members receive:
- Free postage and packing on anything ordered from the Featherstone catalogue
- A 15% discount voucher upon joining which can be used to buy any number of books from the Featherstone catalogue
- Members price of £4.99 on any additional Little Book purchased
- A regular, free newsletter dealing with club news, special offers and aspects of Early Years curriculum and practice
- All new Little Books on approval - return in good condition within 30 days and we'll refund the cost to your club account

Call 020 7458 0200 or email: littlebooks@bloomsbury.com for an enrolment pack. Or download an application form from our website:
www.bloomsbury.com

The **Little Books** series consists of:

All through the year
Bags, Boxes & Trays
Big Projects
Bricks & Boxes
Celebrations
Christmas
Circle Time
Clay and Malleable
Materials
Clothes and Fabric
Colour, Shape & Number
Cooking from Stories
Cooking Together
Counting
Dance
Dance Music CD
Dens
Discovery Bottles
Dough
Drama from Stories
Explorations
Fine Motor Skills
Free and Found
Fun on a Shoestring
Games with Sounds
Gross Motor Skills
Growing Things
ICT
Investigations
Junk Music
Kitchen Stuff

Language Fun
Light and Shadow
Listening
Living Things
Look and Listen
Making Books and Cards
Making Poetry
Maps and Plans
Mark Making
Maths Activities
Maths from Stories
Maths Outdoors
Maths Problem Solving
Maths Songs & Games
Messy Play
Minibeast Hotels
Multi-sensory Stories
Music
Nursery Rhymes
Opposites
Outdoor Play
Outside in All Weathers
Painting
Parachute Play
Persona Dolls
Phonics
Playground Games
Prop Boxes for Role Play
Props for Writing
Puppet Making
Puppets in Stories

Resistant Materials
Rhythm and Raps
Role Play
Role Play Windows
Sand and Water
Science through Art
Scissor Skills
Seasons
Sequencing Skills
Sewing and Weaving
Small World Play
Sound Ideas
Special Days
Stories from around the
world
Story bags
Storyboards
Storybuilding
Storytelling
Time and Money
Time and Place
Topsy Turvy
Traditional Tales
Treasure Baskets
Treasure Boxes
Tuff Spot Activities
Washing lines
Woodwork
Writing

All available from
www.bloomsbury.com